INSIDE THE
COTTON
INDUSTRY

by Marcia Amidon Lusted

Content Consultant

Gaylon D. Morgan

Professor and State Extension Cotton Agronomist
Department of Soil & Crop Sciences
Texas A&M AgriLife Extension Service

Essential Library

An Imprint of Abdo Publishing | abdopublishing.com

abdopublishing.com

Published by Abdo Publishing, a division of ABDO, PO Box 398166, Minneapolis, Minnesota 55439. Copyright © 2017 by Abdo Consulting Group, Inc. International copyrights reserved in all countries. No part of this book may be reproduced in any form without written permission from the publisher. Essential Library™ is a trademark and logo of Abdo Publishing.

Printed in the United States of America, North Mankato, Minnesota
102016
012017

THIS BOOK CONTAINS
RECYCLED MATERIALS

Cover Photo: Adriano Kirihara/Shutterstock Images
Interior Photos: Sun Jin Kim/Rex Features/AP Images, 4; Shutterstock Images, 6, 12, 20, 22–23, 74; Zhang xiuke/Imaginechina/AP Images, 9; North Wind Picture Archives, 14, 26, 33, 34, 37, 44; Jerry Horbert/Shutterstock Images, 18–19; History/Bridgeman Images, 24; Everett Historical/Shutterstock Images, 29, 31, 48, 50; Bettmann/Getty Images, 38; Bygone Collection/Alamy, 41; World History Archive/Alamy, 46; Everett Collection/Newscom, 53; Paul Sakuma/AP Images, 56; Richard B. Levine/Newscom, 60; Alex Hicks Jr./The Spartanburg Herald Journal/AP Images, 62; Michael Buckner/Getty Images, 63; Inga Spence/Science Source, 64; Design Pics Inc/Alamy, 66–67; Red Line Editorial, 69, 91, 96–97; Denton Rumsey/Shutterstock Images, 71; Patrik Stollarz/AFP/Getty Images, 73; Andres Cristaldo/EPA/Newscom, 76; Joerg Boethling/Alamy, 78–79; Anne Chadwick Williams/Zuma Press/Newscom, 81; Ton Koene/Picture-Alliance/DPA/AP Images, 84; James Hardy/Altopress/Newscom, 86; Fashionstock.com/Shutterstock Images, 94; Tripplaar Kristoffer/Sipa/AP Images, 95

Editor: Mirella Miller
Series Designer: Craig Hinton

Publisher's Cataloging-in-Publication Data

Names: Lusted, Marcia Amidon, author.
Title: Inside the cotton industry / by Marcia Amidon Lusted.
Description: Minneapolis, MN : Abdo Publishing, 2017. | Series: Big business |
    Includes bibliographical references and index.
Identifiers: LCCN 2016945200 | ISBN 9781680783704 (lib. bdg.) |
    ISBN 9781680797237 (ebook)
Subjects: LCSH: Cotton textile industry--Juvenile literature. | Cotton trade--
    Juvenile literature. | Cotton products--Juvenile literature.
Classification: DDC 338.4--dc23
LC record available at http://lccn.loc.gov/2016945200

Contents

1 | THE UNIVERSAL FIBER

In April 2016, the Massachusetts Institute of Technology (MIT) created a new nonprofit group to speed up breakthroughs in fiber science and advance the development of new "smart" fabrics. The nonprofit group, the Advanced Functional Fabrics of America (AFFOA), worked to improve the fabric used in clothes, transportation, and electronics. Developments would enhance protective clothing worn by soldiers and first responders. Part of the group's mission is to develop fabrics that have applications beyond clothing. This includes bands of sensitive cloth that monitor unborn babies, fabrics used in creating touch-sensitive skin for robots, and even special knitted fabrics that are made into an exoskeleton that helps rehabilitate injuries. AFFOA also hopes to fund research into embedding fibers with special properties for communication or energy generation and creating new digital tools for designing clothing, such as a machine that knits special fabrics in a process similar to a 3D printer. Scientists are already working on cotton fibers coated with gold nanoparticles. The fibers could be used to sense toxic gases and other pollutants.

These new fabrics include one of the oldest fibers known to humans: cotton. So why are researchers using cotton, instead of inventing a completely new fiber? Cotton is one of

Researchers are creating fabrics that can store energy to charge cell phones and other electronic devices.

Most clothing sold is made from cotton. the most versatile fibers for clothing and other uses. It is an excellent material for fabric innovations.

Cotton is breathable and natural, takes dye colors easily, and is comfortable instead of scratchy next to the skin. Cotton and its by-products are used in ways that might not be as obvious as a T-shirt or a pair of jeans. Cottonseed is used in feed for dairy and beef cattle. Cottonseed oil, which is produced when cottonseed is crushed, is an ingredient in many foods, such as French fries and potato chips. It is also in cereal, baked goods, mayonnaise, soap, and cosmetics. Cotton fibers are used to weave furniture upholstery. Cotton is in the cloth that covers hardcover books, and in the paper pages inside those books. Cotton is used to weave fishnets, create coffee filters, and make bandages. It is the primary ingredient in paper money. Cotton has so many uses that at any time, most of the world's population is eating or using something that came from the cotton plant.

One Bale of Cotton

A cotton bale weighs approximately 480 pounds (218 kg).[1] According to the National Cotton Council of America, one bale can produce the following number of products in any one of these categories:

215	Pairs of jeans
249	Bedsheets
690	Terry cloth bath towels
765	Men's dress shirts
1,256	Pillowcases
3,085	Diapers
4,321	Socks
21,960	Women's handkerchiefs
313,600	$100 bills[2]

TRADING COTTON

Because of its popularity and versatility, cotton is a heavily traded commodity, and it is extremely important to world trade. Cotton is grown in more than 100 countries. Depending on the year, cotton makes up approximately 30 percent of the world's fiber trade output.[3]

Cotton is processed in a Chinese factory to keep up with the high demand of cotton exports from the country.

Because it is grown, imported, and exported by many countries around the world, cotton is also a politically important crop. It can have a large effect on a country's economy, especially in developing countries. Cotton is a significant part of some countries' gross domestic product (GDP), which is the total value of all goods and services produced in a country in one year. The GDP is a primary indicator of a country's economic health.

The T-Shirt

People often wear T-shirts, either in solid colors or with a design or slogan on them. This wardrobe staple has a long history. Back in 1880, sailors in the US Navy were issued undershirts that reached their elbows and fell to hip length. When the shirts were laid out on a flat surface, they resembled the letter T, which is how they got their name. Farmers, miners, and construction workers started wearing T-shirts because they were lightweight and better to wear in hot weather than button-up shirts. They were also inexpensive and easy to clean. One of the first printed T-shirts appeared in 1942, when a man wearing a T-shirt printed with the Army Air Forces Gunnery School was shown on the cover of LIFE magazine. Soon after, Mickey Mouse started appearing on T-shirts. By the 1950s, T-shirts became fashion statements. They featured advertising slogans, city or state names, protest images, art, or other images and words.

Cotton provides governments with tax income, which countries receive from cotton growers or as taxes on imports and exports. Cotton has been extremely important in the development of many African countries, as well as Asian nations including Kazakhstan, Uzbekistan, Tajikistan, Kyrgyzstan, and Turkmenistan.

In 2015, the value of all cotton exported worldwide was more than $54 billion. In the United States alone, the cotton trade was worth more than $6 billion.[4] It was one of the country's most important crops because the money spent to grow and harvest it also created income for the processing, shipping, and textile production industries. This means the original value of the cotton crop has value added to it with every new process, piece of equipment, or industry that receives money from handling it. US farmers spend approximately $5 billion each year for the tools,

Cotton Is Money

In the United States, paper currency is made from 75 percent cotton and 25 percent linen.[5] This makes the bills more durable than if they were made from wood pulp. It also allows the US Mint to insert security fibers and other security features into the bills. These features include security ribbons woven into the bill, which glow pink under ultraviolet light, as well as ribbons that create a changing 3D image. Watermarks, which are faint images that are woven into the paper and that are only visible when held up to light, are also possible with cotton paper. In an average year, the US Mint prints six billion bills of all denominations—$1, $5, $10, $20, $50, and $100. That is nearly 22,000 cotton bales. The face value of all these bills combined is more than $219 billion, which means every pound of cotton makes more than $21,000 in bills.[6]

equipment, and services needed to grow cotton.[7] Only China and India grow more cotton than the United States.

In the United States, cotton is grown in 17 states, from Virginia to California. Cotton fields cover approximately 12 million acres (4.9 million ha). US cotton farmers harvest approximately 15 million cotton bales every year, totaling 7.3 billion pounds (3.3 billion kg). Of this crop of cotton, approximately 75 percent is used for clothing. Another 18 percent is used for home furnishings, while 7 percent goes to industrial products. In addition, nearly 5.2 million short tons (4.7 million metric tons) of cottonseed and 90 million gallons (341 million L) of cottonseed oil are also produced.[8]

STABILITY OF THE COTTON INDUSTRY

However, cotton as a trade commodity is somewhat unstable. Part of this is because unlike commodities such as oil or lumber, cotton is vulnerable to good and bad growing seasons. A good crop of cotton might mean there is too much cotton available and prices fall as a result. A bad growing year may result in insufficient cotton, raising prices but also meaning farmers do not have as much to sell. Cotton is subject to quotas under which some countries limit how much cotton can be imported or exported. Other countries impose tariffs on imported cotton. There is the added element of demand, too. In some years there is a greater demand for cotton. But when the global economy is slower and not as many people are buying clothing and home goods, textile manufacturers buy less cotton. It is beneficial for farmers when cotton prices increase, since they get more for their crops. But high cotton prices might force textile manufacturers to use more

The global market for cotton is always changing.

manmade fabrics, and the farmers will lose income from their cotton.

So why should people care about cotton, other than the cost of a new pair of jeans or a bag of potato chips? Cotton is both an important commodity for everyday lives and a big piece of a country's economy, as well as the world's. But even more so, cotton has had a tremendous impact on the history of the United States and the world. This small plant has been responsible for major historic decisions and organizations; it has contributed to settlements, trade routes, and wars; and it played a major role in institutions such as slavery. To understand where the cotton industry is today, it helps to look back at the history of cotton itself, the birth of cotton as an important element of trade, and how the crop has shaped people and governments. That is a lot of history, even for a plant first discovered more than 7,000 years ago.[9]

The Cotton Industry

Approximately 440,000 Americans are employed in the cotton industry.[10] This number includes farmers and laborers who grow and harvest the cotton, but also people who work in other industries related to cotton. There are 3,500 cotton gins, cottonseed mills, warehouses, merchandisers, shipping companies, and textile factories in the United States.[11] Employees clean and deseed raw cotton in gins. They process the cottonseed and crush it for oil in cottonseed mills. Merchandisers sell these products to places such as factories that make food with cottonseed oil or textile factories that spin cotton into cloth. Shipping companies move cotton products from one place to another by ships, trucks, and trains. All of these industries provide many jobs for Americans across the country.

2 | ANCIENT THREADS

Cotton is an ancient fiber. It grows wild in many places on Earth, but humans have been using and growing it for thousands of years. Archaeologists found the earliest evidence of cotton in a cave in Mexico. They found pieces of cloth and cotton bolls that were approximately 7,000 years old.[1] In the Indus Valley, which is in modern Pakistan, archaeologists found cotton cloth that dates to 5,000 years ago. Ancient Egyptians and Peruvians were also familiar with cotton. Scraps of cotton material have been found in their tombs. But most historians believe India, where cotton grows naturally, was the first place where people cultivated cotton as a crop. An ancient Hindu hymn mentions "threads in the loom."[2] Historians believe this meant cotton had been harvested and made into cloth.

Varieties of cotton were native to North and South America. In the United States, Native Americans grew cotton in the early 1500s. The Hopi worshiped a goddess who was believed to spin and weave cotton. Spanish and Portuguese conquistadors came to the Americas beginning in the 1400s. They were soldiers who explored new places and conquered the native people. Between 1540 and 1542, when the Spanish conquistador Francisco Vázquez

Early people living in Mexico may have been the first humans to use and spin cotton.

de Coronado explored what is now the southwest part of the United States, he mentioned seeing the Hopi growing cotton. The Spanish settlers in Florida also grew cotton in approximately 1556. Colonists in Virginia were growing cotton by 1607.

GROWING COTTON

There are several species of wild cotton, but not all of them are good for cultivating or spinning. South American farmers grew cotton that looked similar to a small bushy tree with yellow flowers. This was long-staple cotton. In India, however, farmers grew cotton that looked more similar to a shrub with yellow or purple flowers and produced short-staple cotton. Staples are a way of measuring the length of the cotton fibers the plant produced. In general, long-staple cotton produces softer and more durable products. Eventually, one type of cotton, American Upland, became the dominant cotton grown by US cotton farmers. It can be short-staple or long-staple.

American Upland grows from seed, which takes approximately five to ten days to sprout and begin

··

Cotton for the King

In ancient Mexico, cotton was known as *ichcatl*, and it was the most valuable crop people grew. When the cotton fibers were mature, they were plucked, and the seeds were removed by hand. Then the fibers were handspun into thread and woven on a backstrap loom, which was attached to the weaver on one end and a tree on the other end. The cloth the weavers produced was strong and flexible, and it could be dyed blue or red with cochineal or indigo. Cochineal was a red dye produced from the small cochineal insect, and indigo was a plant that produced a deep blue dye. However, the weavers did not keep most of the cloth they made. By law, they had to pay a tribute of a certain amount of cloth to their ruler.

growing. It grows into a green, bushy plant three feet (1 m) tall.[3] The plant sprouts flower buds called squares approximately two months after planting. These squares become blossoms that start out creamy white, and then darken to pink and eventually a dark red after being pollinated. After the blossoms wither and fall off the plant, they leave green pods called cotton bolls, which are shaped similarly to small footballs. The bolls are a type of fruit because they contain cottonseeds. The bolls grow and start to swell as the cottonseed and attached fibers mature. After the seeds and fibers have matured, the boll splits open. By the time the cotton plant reaches maturity, approximately one and a half months after the boll appears, it will contain 500,000 cotton fibers. One plant can grow as many as 100 bolls.[4]

CLIMATE AND PESTS

Cotton plants require warm climates and a long growing season. In the United States, the region where cotton grows best is known as the Cotton Belt. The Cotton Belt includes Alabama, Arizona, Arkansas, California, Florida, Georgia, Kansas, Louisiana, Mississippi, Missouri, New Mexico, North

The Vegetable Lamb

When medieval Europeans first encountered cotton plants, they thought the plant was a mixture of a plant and an animal. They called it a "vegetable lamb" since lambs grew fleece. The Vegetable Lamb became a popular myth, often written about in travel books. Author Becky Crew wrote about this myth:

> Medieval texts described two varieties of the Vegetable Lamb—the first produced little naked, newborn lambs inside its pods, and the other had a life-sized lamb, with bones, blood and flesh, attached by its belly button to a short plant stem. This stem was extremely flexible, so allowed the tethered lamb to graze on the vegetation around it. Once all the vegetation was eaten, or if the stem broke, the lamb would die.[5]

Carolina, Oklahoma, South Carolina, Tennessee, Texas, and Virginia. Internationally, the largest cotton-growing regions are found in China, India, Pakistan, Uzbekistan, Turkey, Brazil, and Australia.

At maturity, the cotton fibers dry and fluff out.

Cotton plants are susceptible to many different insect pests. The pests include the cotton aphid and the cotton bollworm, as well as several kinds of caterpillars, plant bugs, mites, thrips, stinkbugs, and whiteflies. But for many years, the most devastating insect for the cotton plant was the boll weevil.

In 1892, this pest migrated to the United States from Mexico. The female boll weevil uses its mouthparts to poke a hole in the cotton plant's boll and deposit up to 300 eggs.[6] As a result, boll weevil–infested cotton was destroyed. The effects were so severe that cotton producing organizations and the

When the boll weevil eggs hatch, the larvae destroy the bolls, which turn brown and fall off.

US government launched a program to eradicate the boll weevil in 1978. The program used insecticides, encouraged crop rotation, destroyed boll weevil habitats, and developed new varieties of cotton that matured and produced fruit earlier than older varieties.

MODERN PEST MANAGEMENT

Today, farmers in the United States use a system called integrated pest management to manage pests that affect yield and fiber quality. This includes introducing populations of good insects to control the population of damaging insects. Using a pest's natural predator is one form of what is known as biological control. Other modern methods of biological control include releasing sterile populations of the most damaging insects. This results in fewer pests being bred.

Some cotton varieties have been specially bred to be less attractive to insects. Crops are also bred to require a shorter growing season, so there is a better chance of a crop reaching maturity before insects can do too much damage. Pesticides are also used to control insects, but in the United States, they must be approved by the US Environmental Protection Agency to make sure they do not harm humans, animals, or the environment.

PROCESSING COTTON

Once the cotton bolls have matured, cotton must be harvested and processed. In the past, cotton was always picked by hand, and in some parts of the world, it still is. But now in the United States, cotton harvesting is done with either a picker or a stripper machine. A picker has spindles that

twist the cotton from the open bolls. Small rollers covered with wire teeth, called doffers, then remove the cotton from these spindles. Inside the machine, air blows the picked cotton into the picker's basket.

Stripping machines are similar. They use rollers with brushes to knock the open cotton bolls from the plants and drop them onto a pneumatic conveyor. Inside the stripper, cotton is cleaned of sticks and burrs and blown into a large basket. Strippers work best in dry climates. One of their downsides is that they accumulate more debris, such as sticks and stems.

3 | COTTON AND SLAVERY

Arab traders brought samples of cotton into Europe in 800 CE, whetting Europeans' appetites for more, but there was no regular source for cotton cloth. It was not until the 1600s that cotton was first imported on a large scale into Europe from India. By 1664, the British East India Company was importing 250,000 pieces of calico- and chintz-patterned cotton cloth into the United Kingdom each year.[1] The English did not yet know how to make cotton cloth with these fine patterns woven into it, but cotton became popular with English clothing makers.

The process to create the colorful patterns was a secret until the mid-1700s, when a French Catholic priest published a step-by-step booklet on how Indian weavers created their patterns. Soon, English mills could weave their own chintz and calico cloth, and they relied on India only to provide them with raw cotton. In the 1700s, the Industrial Revolution in the United Kingdom began, introducing new ways of making goods. Richard Arkwright started a factory system in which spinning and weaving were done with waterpower. Eventually, steam-powered machinery took over. Cities such as Manchester, nicknamed "Cottonopolis," became centers of cotton production.[2]

A port in India where traders came to buy and sell cotton and other goods beginning in the 1600s

A new era of US history began when the United Kingdom began buying cotton from the United States.

At first, the United Kingdom's textile mills were receiving almost all of their raw cotton from India. They made arrangements with Indian farmers to buy their crops. The mills pressured the farmers to plant more cotton, which caused famine in some areas as the cotton crops displaced food crops. Cotton prices also fell while food prices rose in these areas. But the United Kingdom continued buying its cotton from India until the middle of the 1800s, when a new market opened up. The United States was now producing cotton that was stronger, had longer fibers, and cost less. English textile mills had a new source of raw cotton.

In the United States in the 1800s, the importance of cotton to the country's economy gave the crop the nickname "King Cotton."[3] Southern writers and economists used this phrase to sum up how critical cotton was both economically and politically. The United States relied on cotton because it was so profitable. And the United Kingdom relied on US cotton to feed its huge textile industry. The US cotton economy was based on the use of slave labor. Plantation owners

Cotton or Food?

The imbalance between growing more cotton and less food was catastrophic for Indian farmers in the late 1800s. When farmers planted more cotton and not enough food crops, cotton prices fell but food prices rose, so poor farmers could not afford to buy food for themselves and their families. In the 1870s, and again in the early 1900s, millions of Indian peasant farmers died in famines because they could not afford to buy food and were not able to grow it on their own. People who were workers and did not own land had even more difficulty. They were earning less because of competition from workers in other regions, and they had to pay more for their food.

Who Really Invented the Gin?

There is controversy about whether Eli Whitney invented the cotton gin entirely on his own, or if he received ideas and design help from Catherine Green. Green owned a plantation near Savannah, Georgia, where she rented a room to Whitney. Green explained to Whitney how difficult it was to remove cotton seeds, and she suggested he build a machine to do it. This may be as much as she contributed, or perhaps she had an early design for the gin that Whitney refined, since she had more experience with cotton growing and processing. It could also be that Green invented the gin, but because women were not permitted to receive patents in their names at this time, it was Whitney who received the official patent instead. Whitney eventually paid Green some royalties from his patent, which suggests she played a role in the gin's invention.

forced enslaved Africans and African Americans to pick and process cotton.

Small versions of the gin could be cranked by hand, and large versions ran on horsepower or waterpower.

THE COTTON GIN

Separating the seeds from the cotton fiber, or lint, was labor-intensive work. This changed in 1792, when Eli Whitney invented the cotton gin, a device that removed the seeds from cotton mechanically. It had stiff, brushlike teeth that could move through raw cotton and take out most of the seeds. Before the gin, it could take ten hours to remove the seeds from one pound (0.5 kg) of cotton by hand. The cotton gin could process 1,000 pounds (450 kg) of cotton in one day, and it only required human labor to load and unload the cotton and run the machinery.[4]

The cotton gin suddenly made it possible for US plantation owners to process more cotton more quickly, with fewer slave labor hours. In the year the gin was invented, the United States exported

The Triangle Trade

The Triangle Trade is a simplified way to describe the networks for trading slaves, crops, and manufactured goods between Europe, Africa, and the United States and the Caribbean. Slave ships from the United Kingdom arrived in Africa, carrying iron, cloth, guns, and liquor for trade. In Africa, these goods would be exchanged for men, women, and children who had been kidnapped from their homes and forced to become slaves. The slave ships carried them to the Caribbean, where they were sold at slave auctions. Many were then taken to the United States to work on plantations. The money made from the sale of slaves purchased sugar, coffee, and tobacco to be brought back to the United Kingdom.

138,000 pounds (62,600 kg) of cotton. Two years after the device's invention, the number had risen to 1.6 million pounds (725,750 kg).[5]

Slaves became commodities in the South.

While some people thought the cotton gin might bring about the decline of slavery in the South, the opposite was true. Because cotton was now more profitable, plantation owners wanted to grow more of it, which required more slaves to grow and pick the cotton. Slavery became even more important to the South's economy. By 1860, one of every three Southerners was a slave.[6]

A SLAVE ECONOMY

Slavery in the United States started because bringing over workers from Africa was less expensive than using indentured servants from Europe. Indentured servants agreed to work a certain amount of time to pay back the cost of their travel to the United States and would then be given their freedom. The first Africans came to Jamestown, Virginia, in the 1600s, and the numbers soon increased. These Africans were often

servants, not slaves, and they were still considered to be free. But by 1640, at least one African in Jamestown was declared to be a slave in the official records of the colony. White planters felt it was acceptable to enslave Africans for life because they were not Christians and did not have to be treated the way Christians were expected to treat their fellow men.

Cotton was shipped from the South continuously from September through January.

While no one is certain exactly how many enslaved Africans were brought to the United States from Africa, historians estimate the total to be between six and seven million.[7] Slavery quickly spread through the Southern colonies, and slaves worked mostly on indigo, rice, and tobacco plantations before the cotton gin made it lucrative to grow cotton.

Plantation owners believed enslaved Africans were ideal for working on cotton plantations because they had experience in growing sugar and rice crops from living and farming in Africa. They were also unlikely to get malaria and yellow fever, since they often had immunity to these diseases. Soon, it was no longer necessary to purchase enslaved people in Africa. If an enslaved person had a child, then that child was born a slave. The United States soon had a massive population of enslaved workers.

Plantations in the South were many different sizes. Some farmers who had few, if any, slaves grew cotton. Others grew food crops to sell to the owners of large plantations, since these owners often used their fields exclusively for cotton. No matter the size of the farm or plantation, it took a great deal of labor to grow cotton. The land had to be sculpted into ridges, using horse-drawn

machinery to level the soil. Debris needed to be raked out and then furrows needed to be dug. Old cotton stalks from the previous crop had to be removed.

Slaves applied fertilizer to the land in February and March, and the fields were ready for planting in April. Planting the cottonseeds was done by hand, and once the cotton plants sprouted, they had to be thinned. The area between the rows was frequently weeded. Slaves carried out all of these tasks. The cotton plants bloomed around mid-June, when they were 6 to 12 inches (15 to 30 cm) tall.[8] The cotton bolls opened around late July or early August. Picking began in late August. The cotton was taken to a gin after picking, then taken to cotton markets in larger cities and sold to textile factory owners, merchants, and agents, who would then sell it in the United States or to foreign countries.

LIFE AS A SLAVE

Life for slaves on a cotton plantation was unrelenting work. They lived in small shacks on the plantation, and most able-bodied male slaves worked from sunup to sundown. Female slaves worked in the fields or as domestic servants in the plantation owner's house. Children were typically put to work in the home at an early age, then sent to the fields between the ages of eight and twelve. They were generally forbidden from learning how to read and write.

Enslaved people were subjected to brutal physical abuse. In addition to the bodily harm caused by unrelenting labor in the fields, slaves could be beaten, whipped, or even killed for a minor infraction or for no reason at all. Since they were considered the owner's property, there were no legal repercussions for such torture and murder.

Slaves were controlled with a strict code of behavior, which varied from state to state but generally had much in common. These codes made it legal for slaves to be treated poorly. For example, a slave could be used as a prize in a contest, a gift, collateral for a loan, or as a bet in gambling. Slaves could not carry guns, nor could they do business with anyone unless their master had given permission. Their marriages were not considered valid, and owners could split families up to sell them. Anyone who broke one of these codes could be fined or jailed.

The slavery and plantation systems worked well for the Southern cotton industry, but it perpetuated the inhumane enslavement of Africans. The issue of slavery in the United States would become increasingly divisive in the coming years. Many Northerners sought to end the practice, while in the South people clung to slavery and defended it as a traditional way of life. The dispute would contribute significantly to a brutal civil war that would settle the question for good. The war's outcome would also set the stage for the transition into cotton's modern era.

4 | THE US COTTON INDUSTRY

The increased ability of the South to produce cotton meant many other countries were dependent on the United States for raw cotton. But the North and its textile mills were also a market for cotton. This enabled all of the United States to profit from the cotton economy—and exploit the system of slavery—not just the South.

US textile mills owed their start to the industrial spying of Samuel Slater. Slater was born in England in 1768. When he was young, he began work as an apprentice in a cotton mill. He advanced to become a supervisor, where he spent much of his time with the mill machinery designed by Richard Arkwright. Arkwright had developed a factory system that used waterpower to power the mill machinery and divided tasks among a group of workers to speed up the process.

The United Kingdom did not want Arkwright's technology to leak to other countries. It wanted to be the only country with the knowledge to weave cloth quickly, allowing it to dominate the cotton cloth market. For this reason, the United Kingdom refused to let anyone leave the country if they had ever worked in a textile mill. Slater, however, decided

Samuel Slater further developed Arkwright's waterpower factory system in the United States.

he could make a great deal of money by starting his own mills in the US colonies, using Arkwright's designs. Slater disguised himself as a farmer and managed to leave the country undetected. However, the British textile community later discovered his theft, and for many years he was referred to as "Slater the Traitor."[1]

Child Labor

Slater's first mill employed children between the ages of seven and twelve, although there were some workers as young as four years old.[2] By 1830, more than half of the mill workers in Rhode Island were children, working long hours for less than $1 a week.[3] Child labor was more widely accepted at this time, since children routinely began working on their family farms at a young age. Slater reasoned that his mill machinery was simple enough that children could operate it. However, children working in mills were exposed to a dirty and dangerous work environment and long hours. Many never attended school.

Slater could not carry any written plans or designs with him. Instead, he memorized the design of Arkwright's water-powered spinning frame, which was called a water frame. Slater arrived in the United States in 1789, and the next year, he built a textile mill in Pawtucket, Rhode Island. It was not easy to reproduce a machine from memory. Slater's mill workers had to create many of the components they needed on-site, but eventually his mill was running with water-powered spinning machines.

Slater Mill was a success. The mill attracted workers and their families, and Slater allowed them to live on the mill site. In 1803, Slater and his brother built a village around the mill, called Slatersville. The village included boardinghouses where single workers could live and tenement houses

Slater's water-powered spinning machine easily spun raw cotton into yarn for weaving.

for workers who had families, as well as a company store. This system of building villages where textile workers could live and work became known as the Slater System. Soon, other entrepreneurs were imitating the system throughout New England. Among them was businessman and investor Francis Cabot Lowell.

LOWELL'S IMPROVEMENTS

Lowell took Slater's system and improved it by putting all of the processes for going from raw cotton to finished cloth under one roof. Slater's mills spun raw cotton into yarn. Lowell's new mill in Massachusetts spun yarn and also incorporated a water-powered loom. It was a technological improvement over the British power loom, which ran on steam, and it used a refined system of gears and shafts to make the weaving process faster and require less tending by weavers. It also enabled mills to weave patterns more easily into cloth.

Francis Cabot Lowell

Francis Cabot Lowell, born in Massachusetts in 1775, is remembered not only as a smart businessman, but also as a humanitarian. On a visit to the United Kingdom when he was 36, Lowell saw English textile mills and was impressed by them. He returned to Boston determined to create his own mills. He and some of his business associates formed the Boston Manufacturing Company in 1813. They built a mill in Waltham, Massachusetts, incorporating the idea of housing all the processes for weaving cloth under one roof. But he also created a system in which workers were treated well and women were allowed to work in the mills. He ensured his workers were paid in cash and received housing in clean, company-owned boardinghouses.

Lowell also hired young women to work in the mills. They were often as young as ten and were paid less than men for the same jobs, but they lived in clean, safe company boardinghouses. Their lives were strictly regulated, so families did not worry they were sending their daughters to a place where they might behave improperly. Many girls sent their wages home to help their families. As mill workers, the girls had access to religious and educational programs, as well as entertainment to spend their money on. While working as a mill girl meant long hours in an often dirty and dangerous environment, these girls enjoyed much more freedom than they would have at home.

Lowell raised money in a new way as well, selling shares of the Boston Manufacturing

Company. Investors put money into the mills and then received dividends from the profits. This system quickly spread to other US businesses. Lowell died in 1817, but his company flourished. In 1822, the Boston Manufacturing Company built a new mill town on the Merrimack River and named it Lowell. The factory system that Slater began and Lowell perfected helped move New England from a farming economy to a manufacturing one and helped make it competitive in the worldwide cotton textile market.

COTTON DURING THE WAR

The textile industry, from the plantations growing cotton in the South to the mills producing cloth in the North, was deeply affected by the onset of the American Civil War (1861–1865). The Civil War was fought between the Confederate States of America, or the South, and the Union, or the North. The 11 Confederate states left the United States and formed their own country, largely in order to protect their right to continue the institution of slavery. The South was still largely a farming economy, heavily dependent on slave labor, whereas the North had become more industrial. Many Northerners were against slavery.

Literary Mill Ladies

One of the advantages for young women working in the Lowell textile mills was the opportunity for educational programs and access to books. In 1840, a group of young women in Lowell started their own magazine, the *Lowell Offering*. All of its content, including stories, essays, and poetry, was written by mill girls. The *Lowell Offering* became widely popular, and when famous author Charles Dickens visited Lowell, he was impressed and wrote about the magazine for his English audience. The magazine lasted until 1845.

Much of the textile industry in the United States was found in the North.

It was a bloody war in which family members often fought against each other. The North had more people and more equipment for war. It also had more factories, railroads, and food. However, the South had skilled soldiers who were fighting on familiar territory, as most of the war's battles were fought in the South.

The war heavily impacted the cotton and textile industries. Before the Civil War, textiles were the most important industry in the United States. The rise of mills and mill towns drove many people to leave the countryside and move to cities. But most of the industry was concentrated in the North, and the South just supplied the raw cotton to Northern factories.

Burning Cotton

In 1862, less than one year after the Civil War began, Confederate troops were ordered to burn cotton to create a shortage and force important customers, such as the United Kingdom, to recognize the Confederacy. An 1862 Confederate song said, "Burn the cotton! Burn the cotton! From its ashes there shall spring, Herald's of a newborn nation, claiming still that 'Cotton's King!'"[5] When the Union troops invaded the South, they also burned any cotton fields they found, to prevent the Confederacy from selling the cotton to pay for its war efforts.

As the war began, the North blockaded Southern ports, preventing supplies from coming in and raw cotton from being shipped out to the United Kingdom. Of course, no raw cotton was going to the northern factories, either. The South believed that, since 80 percent of the United Kingdom's cotton came from the South, the country would support the South in the war.[4] The

During the Civil War, Southern merchants had no way to ship out their cotton to markets around the world.

United Kingdom did not support the South, however, because it did not agree with slavery. The country also had plenty of raw cotton. This meant it could avoid becoming involved in the American Civil War. The United Kingdom had turned to other suppliers instead. The South smuggled some cotton out to Mexico, the Bahamas, and Cuba, where it could be sold to other countries, but overall cotton production in the South fell from 4.5 million bales in 1861 to only 300,000 by 1864.[6] Many farmers could not grow cotton because of the war going on around them.

The Union victory in 1865 ended the practice of slavery in the United States. The cotton industry stopped being propped up by massive amounts of free labor. Cotton was no longer king in the South, and soon the world would turn back to other markets for raw cotton.

The Cotton Famine

The Lancashire cotton mills in the United Kingdom had a four-month supply of cotton stockpiled when the Civil War began. They thought the war would be short, but it dragged on. Lancashire eventually ran out of cotton, and this period was called the "cotton famine."[7] Textile mills in Lancashire and cotton traders in Liverpool shut down their operations because they could not get enough raw cotton. Thousands of mill workers lost their jobs and suffered from extreme hardship. But despite these conditions, workers at the textile mills in Manchester met and voted to continue to support their antislavery position.

5 | A NEW ERA

The American Civil War was over, and cotton's role was changing. The era of large plantations where hundreds of slaves labored to plant, cultivate, and harvest cotton had ended. An entirely new system of labor had to be developed, changing the lives of everyone involved in Southern cotton agriculture. It was a difficult adjustment.

Plantation owners were used to having complete control over their workers and tried to retain this method of running their plantations. But they were met with resistance from the newly freed slaves who wanted to control their own economic lives. Former slaves believed that because they had worked on the land for many years without any payment, they were owed their own land now.

In 1863, President Abraham Lincoln had ordered 20,000 acres (8,090 ha) of confiscated Confederate land to be sold to freed men.[1] In 1865, Union general William Sherman issued a field order that reserved coastal land in Georgia and South Carolina for black settlement. Each black family was supposed to receive 40 acres (16 ha) of land, and be loaned an army mule to help cultivate it.[2] President Andrew Johnson reversed the order one year later and

After the Civil War, many former slaves moved to the North.

Many former slaves continued working in agriculture.

ordered the land to be returned to the people it had been confiscated from, evicting the families who were farming it. Some land was available for sale, but its price put it out of the reach of most former slaves. Blacks protested the loss of land and the federal government's failure to redistribute Southern land equally between whites and blacks.

Many poor white farmers had suffered economically during the war. Before the war, they had concentrated on growing food for their families. Now that the war was over, many decided to grow cotton on their own as a way to make money.

SHARECROPPING

While plantations for other crops were run using paid workers, cotton production began to run on a new system, called sharecropping. Plantation owners provided a plot of land to a farmer and his family. In exchange for the sharecropper's labor in planting and growing cotton, the landowner would give the farmers a portion of the crop, usually 30 to 50 percent.[3] The landowner often also provided tools, a mule, seed, and even clothing, shoes, and food from the plantation store, but often at very high interest rates. If the sharecropper already had a mule and tools, he might be able to negotiate a larger portion of the crop in return.

Ideally, the sharecropper could make enough money to pay for land of his own. The reality, however, was that the system benefitted the landowner. With nothing put down in writing, and many poor farmers who were illiterate, it was easy for a landowner to claim he had provided goods in excess of what the laborer's crop paid. The landowner controlled everything, supervising the production of the cotton crop, controlling the weighing and marketing, and monitoring the recordkeeping.

Sharecropping families might have had to buy food and clothing on credit from a local merchant, so any money they made was already spent to repay that credit. Families worked hard but sank deeper into a cycle of poverty every year, continuing to work for the landowner because they owed him money. David Jordan, a Mississippi state senator whose parents were sharecroppers in the early 1900s, said of his family's experience:

Contract Labor

In 1865, the US government established the Freedmen's Bureau to help people who had been enslaved transition to freedom. It gave out food to people displaced by the war, established schools and hospitals, and supervised the development of a contract labor system. This system was supposed to negotiate labor deals between landowners and former slaves. It involved black workers signing a contract with a white plantation owner, promising to work for a period of time. At the end of that period, the owner would reconcile what was owed to the worker for his part of the crop, and what was owed to the owner for food and equipment that had been provided to the worker on credit. However, many black workers resented this system and refused to participate in it. Landowners often took advantage of their contract labor, and many workers were never able to make any money at all. Sharecropping replaced the contract labor system.

We'd get $12 per bale and we had to pick hard in order to have money to buy food during that season. If we had a rainy week where we couldn't pick at all, then we would have no money. We would have to go get food and [other necessities] on credit. Some came out in the hole five or six times and they never did get out of the hole. So what happened, they caught the midnight train or bus and headed to Chicago and [the landlord] never found 'em, 'cause that was the only way to get out of that miserable situation.[4]

A white landowner weighs a day laborer's picked cotton in Texas.

NEW TECHNOLOGIES AND DEMAND

Sharecropping survived as a system until the mid-1900s, when most sharecroppers left farms to work in factories and other industries in larger cities across the United States. Landowners began using new technologies, such as tractors and mechanical cotton pickers, which made it possible to farm cotton with fewer laborers. The soil in some areas

of the South was being depleted by overuse and becoming less productive, so cotton production shifted toward Texas. During the late 1920s, the United States produced 50 percent of the world's cotton, but as new technologies developed and spread around the world, other countries began producing larger shares.[5] New fertilizers, pesticides, and water management methods made it possible to grow cotton in places that had never before been suitable, such as Australia.

Weevils to Peanuts

In the town of Enterprise, Alabama, there is a statue dedicated to the boll weevil. Because the boll weevil devastated the cotton crop in Alabama, farmers began to diversify and experiment with other crops. Agricultural scientists such as George Washington Carver of the Tuskegee Institute advised farmers to try crops such as peanuts, soybeans, and sweet potatoes. The farmers listened, and as a result, in 1917, Coffee County, Alabama, had the largest peanut harvest in the country. Enterprise erected the statue to the boll weevil in 1919, with an inscription that reads: "In profound appreciation of the boll weevil and what it has done as the Herald of Prosperity this monument was erected by the Citizens of Enterprise, Coffee County, Alabama."[6]

World War I (1914–1918) brought with it a temporary high demand for cotton. Cotton was needed for manufacturing uniforms and for making bandages. But prices fell immediately after the war ended. Many farmers gave up on cotton and moved to urban areas to find jobs. The Great Depression, which began in 1929 and lasted until World War II (1939–1945), negatively affected the cotton industry as well. A bumper crop of cotton created a surplus in 1930, and crop prices fell drastically. The South experienced a drought between 1930 and 1931, which reduced the amount of cotton harvested and compounded the devastation caused by boll weevils.

World War II also brought an increase in the demand for cotton, but there was a labor shortage in the United States because men had either gone to fight the war or were working in factories and other industries needed to manufacture war materials. Following World War II, countries such as the Soviet Union increased their production of cotton tremendously by growing it on huge, government-run farms. Even in the United States, the trend was toward fewer, larger farms instead of smaller farms for cotton growing.

Since the onset of the American Civil War, cotton production in the United States has never been as central to the nation's economy as it once was. Textile mills decreased in number, since it became cheaper to produce cloth overseas. Many textile mills, first in the North and then in the South, closed down. Cotton had become an international commodity and the center of major economic competition.

Cotton Present and Future

Cotton that was wholesaled and traded at cotton exchanges in the South during and after the American Civil War was separated into two categories: spot cotton and futures cotton. Spot cotton is an actual bale of cotton in a warehouse or a wharf. Futures cotton was cotton that was bought and sold for future delivery to a specific place and time. Even today, cotton futures are still a big part of trading. They are essentially contracts in which the buyer agrees to take a delivery of a specific quantity of cotton from the seller, at a predetermined price, at a future date. It benefits both buyer and seller because buyers are guaranteed cotton to purchase, and sellers are guaranteed to have a market for their crop.

6 | COTTON CONTINUES GROWING

Clothing and fashion trends have resulted in larger markets for cotton cloth. In 1873, two partners, Levi Strauss and Jacob Davis, created a new type of work pant made from cotton twill cloth dyed indigo blue and reinforced with rivets at places where the pants received the most wear. The pants became one of the most universal and most popular pieces of clothing: jeans. Their cotton twill cloth got the name *denim* because of a similar French fabric. And since indigo was the most common color for jeans, they became known as blue jeans. Until approximately 1915, the biggest manufacturer of denim cloth, and the source for Levi's jeans, was the Amoskeag Mill in Manchester, New Hampshire, but soon Southern mills began manufacturing denim as well.

Jeans became popular, first as work pants, then as fashion. They caught on with teenagers in the 1950s, and the 1970s and 1980s brought designer jeans into fashion. Jeans are still worn all over the world, and the global market for them is estimated at more than $60 billion a year. Ninety-six percent of US consumers own seven pairs of jeans or more.[1] Some Southern cotton mills still make denim fabric, but raw cotton

Blue jeans have been a wardrobe staple ever since the Levi Strauss company began, creating a steady market for cotton.

is more likely to be exported to countries such as Mexico to be made into jeans there, since labor costs are cheaper.

PIMA COTTON

Another cotton industry that flourished in the United States resulted from the popularity of pima cotton. Pima cotton has an extralong, fine fiber, and it usually sells for up to twice as much as upland cotton. The long fibers result in more durable cotton products. Cotton farmers in central California's San Joaquin Valley began growing pima cotton in the 1990s. By 2011, US cotton farmers were the world's biggest producers, planting 306,000 acres (124,000 ha) of pima cotton in one year.[2] They even invested in special roller cotton gins that could preserve the long fiber length when separating the pima cotton from its seeds.

Like all crops grown in arid locations, pima cotton needs a great deal of irrigation water, estimated at 249 billion gallons (943 billion L) each year.[3] California began feeling the effects of severe drought in 2013. As a result, farmers no longer had enough water available for irrigating such thirsty crops.

Cotton Color

During World War II, there was a shortage of dyes used for coloring cotton textiles. Naturally colored cotton plants were cultivated in the Soviet Union and experimented with in the United States. These cotton varieties were naturally light green or brown in color and could be used to weave cloth of the same color without the need for dyes. Now, many small cotton farmers are growing and selling organic cotton in colors other than white, since organic crops and organically sourced clothing have become popular.

Pima cotton was also becoming more vulnerable to insects such as the pink bollworm, which is resistant to some pesticides. Many California cotton farmers shifted their crops from pima cotton back to higher-value crops, such as vegetables and alfalfa, which brought them high profits while using less water.

INDUSTRY CHALLENGES

The cotton industry faced uncertainty in the mid-2010s. In 2014, several actions by China and India forced US cotton farmers to grow less cotton. China began stockpiling cotton beginning in 2011, pushing the levels of cotton stockpiles around the world to new highs. This affected the global demand for cotton and brought down the price. In response, US cotton farmers began growing less cotton, since the global demand was also less. However, India responded by growing a record amount of cotton. India's government offered its cotton farmers a higher minimum guaranteed price for their cotton, which prompted Indian farmers to grow more of it. This made India the world's biggest producer of cotton in 2015, surpassing China. Cotton producers in the United States asked

Nonwoven Cotton

Products made from cotton have traditionally been made by knitting or weaving cotton fibers into fabric. However, there is a growing market for nonwoven cotton products, including disposable diapers, feminine hygiene products, and medical bandages and sponges. The cotton fibers in these products are bonded together by entangling the fibers, either mechanically, with heat, or using chemicals. These nonwoven fabrics are flat, porous sheets, and can have special characteristics such as absorbency, strength, flame resistance, or filtering. Some fabrics are designed to be sterile, encourage blood clotting in wounds, or have antibacterial properties.

Pima cotton is used for premium quality clothing, linens, and other luxury items because its fiber can be knitted into softer, finer fabrics.

the government to increase assistance to farmers through crop subsidies and crop insurance. Without help, the farmers feared many cotton farmers would go out of business. In 2016, the government agreed, issuing large one-time payments to cotton producers.

There has been some good news, especially for textile mills in the southern United States. Some foreign companies are opening mills there. For a long time, mills were closing because manufacturers found it was cheaper to make cloth in countries where workers could be paid much less. But now, as wages for textile workers in China and other places are increasing, US workers and mills are becoming more price competitive. Higher costs for transportation and for tariffs are also making foreign companies decide to establish manufacturing facilities in the United States.

Technology has also made US mills more competitive by increasing efficiency. Modern textile mills are more automated than they used to be. They require fewer workers, but those workers

China Comes to South Carolina

In March 2015, the Keer Group, a Chinese company, opened a new cotton mill in South Carolina. It brought Chinese workers from its mill in Hangzhou to train its new US workers. Because textile production in China has become less profitable due to rising labor and energy costs, the Keer Group is taking advantage of its US location to find workers looking for manufacturing jobs. South Carolina and US governments have given the company grants and tax breaks to entice it to set up mills in the South. At least 20 Chinese textile manufacturers have now set up mills in North and South Carolina, and companies from India are doing the same.[4]

A textile mill employee checks the material at a plant in South Carolina.

need to have technology skills. There is also an increase in products made from cotton that are not woven, such as diapers, wipes, and filters. These are made from fibers that are compressed, heated, or tangled, such as felt fabric.

All of these factors make US textile mills more attractive. If there are more mills in the United States, it may also be beneficial for mills to buy their cotton domestically as well. Mills can pay lower prices for cotton because it does not have to be shipped from overseas, and farmers benefit from a domestic market for their cotton crops. However, the issues facing the cotton industry go beyond simply supply and demand for cotton goods. There are other factors at work, too.

Cotton Inc. hosts numerous events throughout the year promoting cotton.

COTTON INC.

In 1960, 78 percent of all textile products sold in retail stores were made from cotton. But with the invention of more synthetic fabrics, that percentage had fallen to 34 percent by 1975.[5] As a result, cotton producers formed Cotton Incorporated, a not-for-profit company focused on marketing and research for the cotton industry. Thanks to the efforts of Cotton Inc., cotton's share of the textile market has risen to 60 percent.[6] It helps create more demand for cotton through advertising, such as its famous "Cotton: The Fabric of Our Lives" advertising campaign. It sponsors research to help producers grow more and better cotton and find ways to make cotton more profitable. Cotton Inc. also works to find new markets. It educates cotton growers about issues such as environmental impact, sustainability, and new technologies, and provides technical assistance and training. It gives consumers information about cotton, as well as lesson plans and resources for teachers and students.

7 | COTTON TODAY

Cotton producers in the United States will always be in competition with producers from other countries. Sometimes those countries, such as China and India, have the advantage. And sometimes US producers do, as the recent interest in foreign companies opening textile mills in the southern United States shows. This back-and-forth will continue for as long as people are growing, processing, and using cotton products in their lives.

Cotton will continue to be subject to government regulations, tariffs, and policies, with programs that sometimes subsidize farmers growing cotton, especially in years of low prices. The Chinese government often limits the import or export of cotton, depending on the amount it produces and has in reserve. This can affect US farmers and producers who import or export cotton to and from China. The US government helps cotton farmers by paying part of the cost of crop insurance to protect them from things that might reduce their production, such as drought and other natural disasters. India has a minimum price support program for farmers, which guarantees they will always receive a set minimum price for their cotton, even if the worldwide price is lower.

The global market greatly affects cotton farmers and their crops.

Planting machines ensure the cottonseeds are planted uniformly in precise rows.

COTTON PRODUCTION TODAY

Modern cotton production is much different from the methods used before mechanization. Everything, from planting to processing, is much more automated than it once was. Cotton has the longest growing season of any annually planted crop in the United States. Preparing the soil and planting the cottonseeds is done with planting machines. To minimize competition for water, nutrients, and light as cotton grows slowly during the spring, farmers use herbicides and cultivators between the rows to remove weeds.

Cotton may also need irrigation, depending on where it is being grown. Irrigation helps guarantee a good cotton crop and increase yields. However, 65 percent of the cotton in the United States is grown without irrigation.[1] Cotton grown in Arizona and California generally requires irrigation. Irrigation is done using large spans of sprinklers that pivot from the center of the fields. The most efficient water delivery occurs through small buried hoses that deliver water slowly to the soil and plant roots. The kind of irrigation a farmer uses depends on the type of field and its characteristics, as well as the local climate.

One Cotton T-Shirt

It can take a lot of water to grow cotton, depending on what part of the United States it is grown in. Irrigated cotton grown in the West requires 713 gallons (2,700 L) of water to grow enough cotton for one shirt.[3] But there are other, less obvious needs for water during the lifetime of one cotton T-shirt. There is the water needed to keep the shirt clean. Using a dryer to dry the shirt takes five times as much energy as washing it, which adds to the shirt's carbon footprint.[4] There are other energy costs as well. The raw cotton must be transported to the factory where the shirt is made, then the finished shirt is shipped to where it will be sold.

HARVESTING COTTON

Harvesting is a matter of picking the cotton when it is ready but before it can be damaged by bad weather. Most harvesting machines pick the cotton, then make it into round modules, which are compact units of compressed cotton that look similar to giant marshmallows with a plastic coating. The modules are dropped off the back of the harvester and left in the field, where they are loaded into a truck to be taken to the gin. One module can weigh up to 5,000 pounds (2,300 kg).[2] The modules are unloaded into the gin and pulled apart. The cotton is put through lint cleaners to separate out debris such as sticks, burrs, and leaves, and then it is put through huge dryers to remove moisture. This makes ginning easier and prepares the cotton for safe storage.

Specific types of gins are used for specific types of cotton. Upland, shorter-staple cotton is ginned using a saw gin. This gin has a circular saw that grips the cotton fibers and pulls them through narrow slots. These slots are too small for cottonseeds to pass through, so the fibers are pulled from the seeds, leaving the detached cotton fibers.

This saw ginning process is too rough for cotton with a long staple and will result in broken and short fibers. Long-staple cotton must be ginned with a roller gin. A roller bar grabs the fibers and pulls them under a rotating bar. This bar has gaps that are too small for seeds. Because long-staple cotton is easier to separate from its seeds, this process cleans it easily.

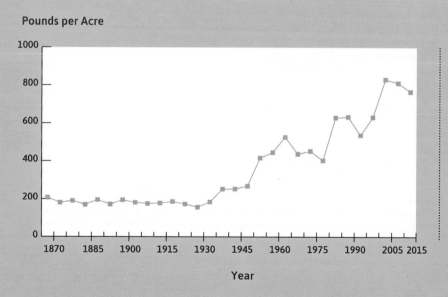

US Cotton Yields

US cotton yields per acre have improved significantly over the past few decades, thanks to a mixture of improved technology and refined farming techniques. These factors have also dramatically increased the production efficiency, lowering the number of hours needed to process each bale of cotton.

The cleaned cotton, no matter which kind it is, is now called lint, and it is pushed using air through a series of pipes to a press. The press compacts it into bales. A standard bale is 55 inches (140 cm) tall, 28 inches (71 cm) wide, and 21 inches (53 cm) thick.[5]

Classing

The fineness of a cotton fiber is important because it determines what a fiber can be used for. Fine cotton fibers make yarn for weaving. It also matters what color the cotton is, because very white cotton is more valuable than cotton that has yellowed in the fields before it was harvested. The amount of trash, such as cotton leaves and stems, that is found in a cotton bale is also important, since the textile mill that purchases the bale will have to remove all the trash before using the cotton. The strength of the cotton fiber determines what fabrics made from that fiber will be like. Longer, finer fibers can be used in luxury fabrics, but they are thinner and less durable. Longer, stronger fibers create fabric that is thicker and lasts longer.

BALE CLASSES

Bales of US cotton lint have to be classed. The lint sample is collected immediately prior to the bale being pressed, and a sample is sent to a US Department of Agriculture Classing Office. An expert classer and calibrated machines class the sample from each bale according to the international standards for the strength of its fiber, the staple length, the uniformity of the fibers, the color, anything in the bale that is not a fiber, and the fiber's fineness. The classer determines this using technical instruments and their own expert knowledge. Not all countries class their cotton, but doing so makes the product more attractive to buyers, since they know what they are getting.

Once the bales of cotton have been classed, a classing card is attached to the bale. Growers

The bales are placed inside a waterproof plastic bag and sealed.

can sell their cotton crop right after it has been ginned and classed, but because cotton is not perishable, they can store it in a warehouse in the hope of later selling it for a better price. They may also have sold it in advance on the futures market, which means it already has a buyer. Because cotton crops can vary in amount and quality worldwide from year to year, the price for cotton can also vary widely based on fiber quality characteristics. In a year in which not as much cotton is grown, bales of cotton can be sold at a higher price. If it is a good year for cotton and almost the entire crop is of a higher quality, then average quality cotton will sell for less than usual.

Types of Cotton

What are the different grades of cotton used for? Mass-produced fabrics and goods, and things that contain cotton blends, are usually made with low- to medium-grade cotton. Higher grades of cotton, which have longer staple fibers, are used for high-quality shirts and bedding. One high-grade cotton is Egyptian cotton, which has grown along Egypt's Nile River for hundreds of years. Other high-grade cottons are pima, American Egyptian, and Sea Island cottons.

Higher-quality lint is always in high demand.

Fair trade gives farmers an alternative way to sell their cotton.

There is also a classification for fair trade cotton, which usually comes from countries where small farmers need more help to be competitive with large farming operations. Fair trade is a certification that includes three standards: economic, social, and environmental sustainability. Its mission is to "provide a framework for a sustainable approach to production that can have long-term economic, social, and environmental benefits for farmers and their communities."[6] In exchange for meeting the fair trade standards, farmers are guaranteed a minimum price for their seed cotton and an additional fair trade premium "for farmers to invest in strengthening their organizations, developing their businesses and improving the infrastructure of their communities."[7]

8 | COTTON AND THE ENVIRONMENT

There are continuing questions about whether modern methods of growing cotton are bad for the environment, and whether it is better to wear clothing made from regular cotton, organically grown cotton, or from a synthetic fabric made in a lab or factory. Cotton uses a great deal of water and pesticides. It uses approximately 7 percent of the total amount of pesticides used in the United States.[1] Worldwide, cotton growing uses 16 percent of the world's pesticides.[2] Cotton also uses large amounts of water for irrigation to maximize yields, depending on where and how it is grown. And there are other issues as well. The garment industry, which uses cotton heavily, is responsible for poor working conditions, child labor, and slave labor in many foreign countries. Workers may toil in sweatshops, working long hours in hot, unsanitary conditions, for very little pay. Children, too, may work in these conditions without the opportunity to attend school. Many garment manufacturers have moved their factories to foreign countries so they can pay much lower wages and not have to meet US standards for health and safety in the workplace.

Some environmental groups consider cotton to be a dirty crop because of its heavy pesticide use. New advances, such as genetically modified cotton, have reduced this pesticide use.

Clothing made from organic cotton is increasingly popular.

The cotton industry is working to address some of these issues. There is a growing market for organic cotton, which is grown without synthetic pesticides. Organic status is regulated by the US Department of Agriculture.

Cotton farmers are working to find ways to increase water use efficiency for growing cotton, which is naturally heat- and drought-resistant in many environments. Farmers use 45 percent less irrigation than they did 25 years ago, while obtaining higher yields.[3] Scientists are continuing to research new varieties of cotton that require less water. US farmers are using conservation tillage practices, which means they plow their fields less often. This reduces erosion and lessens the chance of a heavy rainfall washing away the rich topsoil on fields. Above all, cotton producers point out that cotton is a sustainable crop that renews itself with every new growing season. It is also natural and biodegradable, gradually breaking down and returning to the environment as part of the soil. This makes it much more environmentally friendly than synthetic fabrics, which are petroleum-based. Petroleum is a nonrenewable source and is unable to naturally degrade. Similar to plastic, these fabrics will remain in the environment for hundreds of years or more.

Even with competition from synthetic fabrics and foreign cotton growers, and opposition from those who feel cotton growing takes too much of a toll on the environment, the US cotton industry continues to look forward. And it is facing the future with some interesting and innovative approaches.

GMO COTTON

Bt cotton has given a significant boost to India's cotton industry.

Some countries, including China and India, are now growing cotton classified as genetically modified organisms (GMO), and almost 50 percent of the world's crop of cotton is modified.[4] These modifications make the cotton resistant to certain pests and to herbicides. For example, inserting genes from the *Bacillus thuringiensis*, a natural bacterium that lives in soil, creates Bt cotton. This bacterium causes the cotton to produce proteins with insecticide traits. These proteins kill cotton pests such as tobacco budworms and bollworms. Bt cotton is one of the first products produced by biotechnology to protect crops. It was introduced in the United States in 1996. Bt cotton has significantly lowered the amount of insecticides used by US farmers. According to the US Department of Agriculture:

Bt cotton may offer value to the cotton farmer in ways that are hard to measure by short-term economic comparisons. Using insecticides involves complying with certain laws, such as worker protection and pesticide label restrictions. Compliance often makes the grower's job more difficult and increases the risk of consequences arising from noncompliance. Insecticide use in sensitive areas—next to schools, fish ponds, dwellings, medical facilities, roads—can be a concern to the grower and his or her neighbors. If legal and social risks are a concern, Bt cotton may have value to the grower by reducing these risks.[5]

Some farmers use GMO cotton in order to have to spray for weeds and other pests less often.

Many people are concerned about genetically modified crops, particularly food crops. Some worry that these foods may be less safe than ordinary crops, though there is little evidence to back this up. Others argue these crops can affect farmers negatively since GMO seeds are relatively expensive. However, proponents of GMOs point out that GMO crops can save farmers money in the long run by reducing pesticide costs and increasing yields.

A study of cotton farms in China showed the use of genetically modified cotton, which contains the Bt toxin that is lethal to pests such as the cotton bollworm, can increase the numbers of beneficial insects, such as ladybugs, lacewings, and spiders. These natural insect predators, which are not negatively impacted by the Bt protein, can reduce the numbers of pests such as aphids, which are not one of the pests susceptible to the Bt toxin. The natural insect predators are still necessary to reduce the numbers of these pests.

GMO cotton can have negative effects, too. Some genetically modified cotton has been bred to be resistant to an herbicide called glyphosate. This meant farmers could use glyphosate to kill weeds in their fields without harming the cotton. Often, they were also using the herbicide on glyphosate-resistant corn and soybean crops as well. The glyphosate-resistant crops were very effective tools for managing weeds and increasing a farmer's weed management efficiency. However, the repeated use of glyphosate resulted in weeds that were tolerant to glyphosate. These glyphosate-resistant weeds reproduced and became dominant weeds in farmers' fields. Farmers are now returning to a variety of other methods for weed control, such as plowing, tilling, and cycling through different types of herbicides on a rotating basis. Since the development of glyphosate-resistant weeds, farmers have had to increase tillage and adopt more expensive herbicide programs. The result is lower profits for the same amount of cotton.

Cotton's Numbers

Cotton is the most widespread, profitable nonfood crop grown in the world. Approximately 250 million people around the world depend on growing and processing cotton for their livelihoods. In developing countries, almost 7 percent of all labor is related to the cotton industry.[6] In Africa alone, more than 10 million people depend on cotton exports for their money.[7] In 1946, the average cotton farm in the United States was 17 acres (6.9 ha). Now, the average US cotton farm is more than 1,000 acres (405 ha) in size.[8]

A CARBON FOOTPRINT

Finally, environmentalists take into account cotton's carbon footprint. A carbon footprint is the amount of carbon dioxide produced by a person, group, or object. This greenhouse gas may be produced as a result of farming, manufacturing, or transport. When carbon dioxide is released into the air, it traps the sun's heat in the atmosphere. Over time, this process leads to climate change, the gradual warming of the planet.

The carbon footprint of the textile industry is huge, because it includes the footprint of growing the fibers, weed control, harvesting, irrigation, and transporting cotton to the places where it is processed and then used. Organically grown cotton has a smaller carbon footprint than the standard methods of growing cotton. But due to the global scope of the cotton industry, the cost of growing and transporting any cotton crop is a large carbon footprint. Still, the combined carbon footprint of cultivating and processing cotton is lower than that of other popular fibers, including the synthetic fibers polyester and nylon.

As the cotton industry develops new ways to grow cotton and monitors the effects of those methods on the environment, it is also looking to the future. There will be new methods of farming and production, as well as new markets and new products, to keep up with our rapidly changing lifestyles.

9 | COTTON'S FUTURE

While there are many challenges facing the cotton industry, cotton producers and manufacturers are looking to the future with innovative products and new ideas. Often, these products have been developed with help from science. The adoption of new technology, from seeds to harvesting to ginning, have all drastically improved the efficiency of the cotton industry and have kept it competitive. Some of today's innovative cotton products are made up entirely or almost entirely of cotton. Others combine cotton with different fibers. Cotton remains integral to the world's modern fiber industry.

IMPROVING AN OLD FAVORITE

Denim continues to be a wardrobe favorite in the form of blue jeans. But scientists and textile researchers are finding ways to make denim even better. This new generation of denim has qualities that make it more adaptable and durable. The new J-fiber is a combination cotton-polyester fiber wrapped with cotton. It looks similar to denim, but it has more give and resists bagging, which often happens in the hips and knees of regular blue jeans. It also makes it easier to move in blue jeans because it is more flexible. Another fiber, called DualFX, has a polyester-based fiber

Cotton is mostly used for clothing, but it also has uses in a variety of innovative products.

Many innovative fabrics take advantage of cotton's absorbent properties.

combined with cotton. It provides greater stretch. The new COOLMAX polyester fiber is woven into denim and makes it feel cooler against the skin.

Another new fiber, which is a combination of nylon and cotton, is called Cordura. It can be used to make denim more durable and tear-resistant, as well as water-repellent. The fabric still looks and feels like denim. Researchers are also finding ways to make durable denim that regulates temperature by moving moisture away from the skin. Other new denims have hollow-core fibers that can provide insulation in cold climates.

Materials made only from cotton also have innovative features. One involves treating some cotton fibers to make them water-repellent. Combining these with absorbent fibers results in a fabric that wicks away moisture from the skin, keeping the wearer cool while maintaining the softness and comfort of cotton.

Cotton lint has always been known for its ability to absorb water. But scientists have discovered it can absorb other things just as well. Cotton is the main ingredient in a new wall covering that can absorb sound and heat. This wall covering absorbs everyday noises such as airplanes passing overhead and dogs barking, making a home's interior quieter. It also works as insulation, keeping rooms warm during cold weather. And because the wall covering is made from renewable materials, it is sustainable, easy on the environment, and has a low carbon footprint. The only drawback is that it comes in a semiliquid form and must be troweled onto walls by a certified installer.

One company is now manufacturing insulation from recycled cotton blue jeans. It absorbs noise and insulates against heat and cold. Because it is made from cotton, it has no chemical irritants and does not need special handling or warnings labels, unlike other common insulation materials.

ABSORBING OIL

Cotton is good at absorbing oil, too. One important use for it is helping clean up oil spills that pollute water. Scientists at Texas Tech University have discovered that a low grade of cotton, known as low-micronaire cotton, is very effective when made into booms to contain and absorb crude oil. This type of cotton had previously been discounted when sold to the textile industry because it does not take dyes well. But it has a naturally waxy coating that repels water. It also shrinks and can be packed into a small area.

Low-micronaire cotton absorbs the most crude oil because the oil not only sticks to the surface of the cotton, but it also absorbs into the fibers. One pound (0.5 kg) of low-micronaire cotton can pick up 30 pounds (14 kg) of crude oil.[1] As one scientist said, "That low-micronaire cotton, which is the least valuable cotton, can absorb as much crude oil as it does is a breakthrough discovery. It gives us an excellent tool for cleanup of shorelines, animals and ecologically sensitive areas. . . . It's a major discovery from scientific and economic standpoints."[2]

COTTON IN OTHER MATERIALS

Another innovative use for cotton is a new biodegradable packing material called Mushroom Materials. Similar to chemical foams, Mushroom Materials can be molded to fit an object being packed. But unlike synthetic foams, it can be composted after use instead of ending up in a landfill. Mushroom Materials come in two types: Myco Foam and Myco Board. The manufacturing process for these products, which is low-energy in itself, consists of taking agricultural waste such as cotton burrs, cleaning it, and combining it with mycelium. Mycelium is a fine white filament produced by fungi such as mushrooms. The mycelium strands intertwine with the agricultural waste and form a framework, which is broken up and then used for packing material. Computer companies that need protection for fragile and expensive components are already using these packing materials.

Cotton can also be used to make a spray-on hydromulch used in landscaping. The hydromulch controls erosion in places where the ground is freshly seeded and the seeds need protection from being washed away until they sprout. The hydromulch is made from the waste generated by cotton gins, which amounts to approximately 2.5 million short tons (2.3 million metric tons) a year.[3] The mulch is mixed with water and sprayed on. Because cotton is naturally absorbent and biodegradable, it helps hold moisture so plants can sprout quickly and be protected from rain and wind. The mulch itself gradually dissolves and then decomposes into the environment.

Cotton Wipe

Texas Tech University researchers have used cotton's absorbent qualities to create a nonwoven wipe that absorbs and neutralizes the solids and liquids that might be used in chemical warfare. It can also absorb the vapors given off by chemical weapons. The wipe sandwiches a layer of carbon between two layers of cotton. Because it is made from cotton, it does not leave a residue as other types of decontamination products do, and it is biodegradable.

COTTON IN THE MEDICAL FIELD

Medicine has also found new uses for cotton. Cotton was always used for bandages because it is soft, absorbent, and can be bleached easily to become sterile for wound covering. But researchers are now using cotton in a variety of new medical products. One medical dressing uses cotton because it holds in compounds to promote wound healing. One of these substances is chitosan, which is a carbohydrate that comes from the shells of shrimp. Chitosan is a natural clot-promoter and has natural antibiotic qualities. By combining it with a cotton bandage, it can help heal wounds. Researchers are also developing ways to imbed the chitosan compound in cotton fabric for medical gauze, clothing, and hospital bedsheets.

Specially treated cotton fabric could also be used in high-tech military uniforms to help stop blood loss after an injury. The researchers hope to develop what they call a "bandage with a brain."[4] This bandage would target destructive enzymes in a wound, which can break down tissues or cause infections, and soak them up. The bandage would release helpful proteins to use in healing.

ELECTRICITY, CLOTHES, AND OIL

Cotton has the potential to be used in fabrics that can conduct electricity. Researchers at Cornell University developed a new type of cotton fiber coated with tiny particles of matter called nanoparticles. These nanoparticles are conductive, meaning an electric connection can be made inside the fabric simply by tying two of the threads together. And because of the cotton fibers, the fabric remains soft, light, and flexible. Previous attempts at this technology resulted in heavy, stiff, uncomfortable fabrics.

Possible uses for this new fabric include the creation of smart clothing. Smart clothes could monitor heart and breathing rates or even charge mobile devices such as cell phones and gaming

Cotton Usage after Ginning by Weight

Not all cotton is used to make clothing. In fact, the many different components of cotton are used for a wide variety of items.

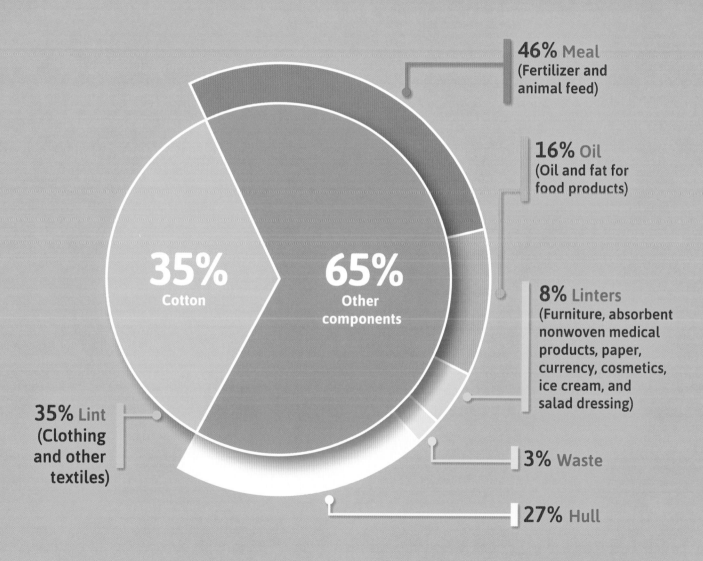

35% Cotton

65% Other components

46% Meal (Fertilizer and animal feed)

16% Oil (Oil and fat for food products)

8% Linters (Furniture, absorbent nonwoven medical products, paper, currency, cosmetics, ice cream, and salad dressing)

35% Lint (Clothing and other textiles)

3% Waste

27% Hull

consoles. Inventors have created clothing that charges electronics by connecting the nanoparticles to a small solar-powered battery and a USB dock. Further advancements in conductive cotton fabric might include analysis of the wearer's sweat to see if there are any signs of disease. Another use might be garments that cool the wearer on hot days.

Chinese researchers have invented a self-cleaning cotton fabric. Using a chemical coating, they created cotton fabrics that clean themselves of stains and odors when exposed to sunlight. The treatment is said to be inexpensive, nontoxic, and environmentally friendly. Other related research includes clothing that can generate heat to keep its wearer warm and clothing that can purify the air around the wearer. Although all of these ideas are still in the development stage, they could someday be available in stores.

MANMADE FIBERS

Cotton is important worldwide, but starting in the mid-1900s, it had serious competition from synthetic, or manmade, fibers. Scientists had been experimenting with synthetic versions of silk fabric since the 1600s. One version debuted at an exhibition in Paris, France, in 1889. This silk, called rayon, was produced commercially not long afterward. Acetate followed, and was used for motion picture film as well as fabric. Both acetate and rayon come from cellulose, a natural fiber from mulberry trees.

In 1931, US chemist Wallace Carothers was researching molecules called polymers. He used plastic chemical compounds to create a new fabric called nylon. Nylon was the first fabric to be made entirely from petrochemicals. It was first used as a fabric for parachutes and women's stockings. After World War II, more synthetic fabrics followed. Acrylic fiber came shortly after, and polyester debuted in the 1950s. In the 1960s and 1970s, more clothing was being made with polyester fabrics, which people like because they do not wrinkle as easily as cotton and linen and do not need to be ironed. There were also fabrics made from blends of cotton and acrylic. Scientists continue to invent new synthetic fabrics, such as spandex and aramid, all of which are made in laboratories instead of being grown in fields. Spandex is still widely used for exercise clothes, and aramid and nylon were used in space suits for the lunar landing in 1969.

Uses for Cottonseeds

Researchers are looking for new uses for cottonseeds and cottonseed oil. Cottonseed oil left over from restaurant kitchens, where it is used for frying, can be recycled into biodiesel used to fuel vehicles. Crushing cottonseeds for oil also produces a protein used in fish and seafood farming. The protein is used to feed shrimp, which are sold as a food source for people.

All of these synthetic fibers and fabrics have been competition for the cotton industry. Many manufacturers prefer synthetic fabrics because they are more consistent in quality. A clothing manufacturer may have to throw away three to eight percent of a cotton bale because it contains short fibers or other defects.[5] But every bit of a bale of nylon or polyester fabric is used with no waste. Economically, it sometimes makes better sense for manufacturers to use synthetic fabrics. Still, cotton's comfort and other properties remain popular with consumers, and manufacturers continue using it either by itself or in blends with other fibers.

Today, many types of clothing are made with cotton fabric.

Despite the challenges it faces in today's world, the cotton industry continues to look to the future. Cotton remains one of the world's most popular fibers. Some 7,000 years after its first known use, almost everyone in the world is still wearing, eating, or using something that contains cotton.

Cargill is involved in every area of the cotton trade.

CARGILL COTTON

One of the biggest cotton companies in the United States is Cargill Cotton. Founded in 1981, Cargill was made up of several cotton trading companies that started in the United States and the United Kingdom in the 1800s. Now the Cargill Company operates as Cargill Cotton UK, which trades cotton from across the world, and Cargill Cotton USA, which trades cotton from the Western Hemisphere.

Cargill has 400 cotton buyers in 50 countries, and they ship cotton all over the world.[6] The company also works with textile mills around the world to supply them with cotton. Its website notes, "Cargill Cotton is present in every cotton producing and consuming region of the world through our network of merchandising, ginning and warehousing operations. We are fluent in every language where cotton is traded and we are available to every time zone in the world."[7]

COTTON PRODUCTION 2015–2016[8]

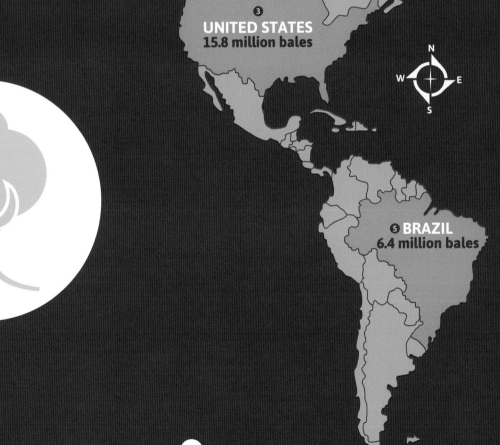

③ UNITED STATES
15.8 million bales

⑤ BRAZIL
6.4 million bales

TURKMENISTAN
1.5 million bales

TURKEY
3.0 million bales

CHINA
21.5 million bales

UZBEKISTAN
3.7 million bales

BURKINA FASO
1.2 million bales

INDIA
27.5 million bales

PAKISTAN
8.0 million bales

AUSTRALIA
2.8 million bales

Timeline

800 CE
Arab traders bring samples of cotton into Europe.

1500s
In North America, Native Americans begin growing cotton.

1664
The British East India Company imports 250,000 pieces of calico- and chintz-patterned cotton cloth into Great Britain.

1790
Samuel Slater builds the first water-powered spinning machine in the United States.

1792
Eli Whitney invents the cotton gin.

1794
The United States exports 1.6 million pounds (725,750 kg) of cotton.

1803
Samuel Slater and his brother build a village around their mill for workers.

1813
Frances Cabot Lowell and some business associates form the Boston Manufacturing Company.

1865

The American Civil War ends in a Union victory, and the practice of slavery is abolished in the United States.

1873

Levi Strauss sells a new type of clothing: blue jeans.

1892

The boll weevil enters the United States from Mexico and becomes a serious threat to the cotton industry.

1931

Wallace Carothers, a US chemist, creates a new fabric called nylon.

1978

The US government launches a program to eradicate the boll weevil.

1996

Bt cotton is introduced in the United States.

2011

US cotton farmers are the world's biggest producers of luxury pima cotton.

2015

The Keer Group, a Chinese company, opens a new cotton mill in South Carolina in March.

Essential Facts

IMPACT ON HISTORY

The cotton industry aided in the settlement of the United States and affected the institution of slavery and the American Civil War. It has also had a major impact on the global textile industry. Today, almost everyone in the world wears, eats, or uses things that are made from cotton. Cotton is no longer used for only clothing items. Technological advancements have utilized cotton in smart fabric, bandages, and home insulation, among other things.

KEY FIGURES

▶ Richard Arkwright develops a new water-powered factory system that enables efficient production of textiles.

▶ Samuel Slater builds upon Arkwright's work and develops textile mills in the United States, building them alongside villages where employees could live and work.

▶ Eli Whitney invents the cotton gin, speeding up the processing of cotton dramatically and contributing to the growth of cotton as an integral crop to the Southern economy.

KEY STATISTICS

▸ By the time the cotton plant reaches maturity, a boll will contain 500,000 cotton fibers. One plant can grow as many as 100 bolls.

▸ A bale of cotton weighs approximately 480 pounds (218 kg).

▸ US cotton production in 2015–2016 equaled 15.8 million bales.

▸ There are 17 US states that grow cotton.

▸ Approximately 440,000 Americans are employed in the cotton industry.

▸ In 2015, the value of all cotton exported worldwide was more than $54 billion.

QUOTE

"Cotton: The Fabric of Our Lives"

—Cotton Incorporated

Glossary

biological control

The reduction of harmful pest populations by introducing natural enemies of those pests into the environment.

boll

The rounded seed capsule of plants such as cotton or flax.

dividend

A sum of money paid regularly to shareholders by a company, from its profits.

genetically modified

A crop containing genetic material that has been artificially changed to produce a desired trait or characteristic.

herbicide

A substance that is harmful to plants and is used specifically for killing weeds.

lucrative

Producing a large profit.

pesticide

A substance or chemical used to destroy insects or other organisms that are harmful to cultivated plants.

staple

A fiber of cotton or wool considered with regard to its length and fineness.

stockpile

To accumulate a large amount of goods or materials, especially to be held in reserve until there is a shortage.

sustainable

A practice that avoids depleting natural resources.

tariff

A set of prices, fees, duties, or taxes on imported or exported goods.

textile

A type of cloth or woven fabric.

Additional Resources

SELECTED BIBLIOGRAPHY

Beckert, Sven. *Empire of Cotton: A Global History*. New York: Knopf, 2014. Print.

"Cotton and Wool." *United States Department of Agriculture*. USDA.gov, 26 May 2016. Web. 1 July 2016.

"Cotton Campus." *Cotton Incorporated*. Cotton Incorporated, 2016. Web. 1 July 2016.

FURTHER READINGS

Cummings, Judy Dodge. *Civil War*. Minneapolis, MN: Abdo, 2014. Print.

Rissman, Rebecca. *A History of Fashion*. Minneapolis, MN: Abdo, 2015. Print.

Rissman, Rebecca. *Women in Fashion*. Minneapolis, MN: Abdo, 2016. Print.

WEBSITES

To learn more about Big Business, visit **booklinks.abdopublishing.com**. These links are routinely monitored and updated to provide the most current information available.

FOR MORE INFORMATION

For more information on this subject, contact or visit the following organizations:

The Cotton Foundation

PO Box 783
Cordova, TN 38088
901-274-9030
http://www.cotton.org/foundation

The Cotton Foundation is a nonprofit group that supports banks, seed companies, chemical and equipment manufacturers, publishers, and others whose success depends at least in part on the US cotton industry.

Cotton Incorporated

PO Box 8006
Cary, NC 27512
919-678-2220
http://www.cottoninc.com

Cotton Incorporated is a research and marketing association for producers and buyers of upland cotton.

National Cotton Council of America

7193 Goodlett Farms Parkway
Cordova, TN 38016
901-274-9030
http://www.cotton.org

The National Cotton Council's mission is to help everyone who is involved in the US cotton industry to compete effectively and profitably both in the United States and overseas.

Source Notes

CHAPTER 1. THE UNIVERSAL FIBER

1. "What Can You Make from a Bale of Cotton?" *Cotton Counts.* Cotton Counts, n.d. Web. 11 July 2016.

2. Ibid.

3. "World Cotton Market." *Cotton Australia.* Cotton Australia, 2016. Web. 10 Aug. 2016.

4. "List of Exporters for the Selected Product: 52 Cotton." *ITC.* International Trade Centre, 2015. Web. 11 July 2016.

5. "$100 Note." *US Currency Education Program.* US Currency, n.d. Web. 11 July 2016.

6. "Cotton and US Currency." *Cotton Counts.* Cotton Counts, n.d. Web. 11 July 2016.

7. "List of Exporters for the Selected Product: 52 Cotton." *ITC.* International Trade Centre, 2015. Web. 11 July 2016.

8. "USDA Coexistence Fact Sheets Cotton." *United States Department of Agriculture.* USDA, Feb. 2015. Web. 11 July 2016.

9. "The Story of Cotton." *Cotton Counts.* Cotton Counts, n.d. Web. 11 July 2016.

10. "Cotton Counts." *Cotton Counts.* Cotton Counts, n.d. Web. 11 July 2016.

11. Ibid.

CHAPTER 2. ANCIENT THREADS

1. "History." *Cotton's Journey.* CottonJourney.com, n.d. Web. 11 July 2016.

2. Ibid.

3. Ibid.

4. Ibid.

5. Becky Crew. "Animal or Vegetable? Legend of the Vegetable Lamb of Tartary." *Scientific American.* Scientific American, 6 Sept. 2013. Web. 11 July 2016.

6. Stephen Yafa. *Cotton: The Biography of a Revolutionary Fiber.* New York: Penguin, 2005. Print. 234.

CHAPTER 3. COTTON AND SLAVERY

1. "Cotton: A History." *New Internationalist Magazine.* New Internationalist, 1 Apr. 2007. Web. 11 July 2016.

2. Ibid.

3. "King Cotton." *Encyclopædia Britannica.* Encyclopædia Britannica, 2016. Web. 11 July 2016.

4. "The Cotton Gin." *Eli Whitney Museum and Workshop.* Eli Whitney Museum and Workshop, n.d. Web. 11 July 2016.

5. "The Crowning of King Cotton." *US History.* USHistory.org, 2016. Web. 11 July 2016.

6. "The Cotton Gin." *Eli Whitney Museum and Workshop.* Eli Whitney Museum and Workshop, n.d. Web. 11 July 2016.

7. "Slavery in America." *History.com.* A&E Networks, 2009. Web. 11 July 2016.

8. "King Cotton." Home of the American Civil War. CivilWarHome.com, 16 Feb. 2002. Web. 11 July 2016.

CHAPTER 4. THE US COTTON INDUSTRY

1. Stephen Yafa. *Cotton: The Biography of a Revolutionary Fiber.* New York: Penguin, 2005. Print. 77–78.

2. Amelia Grabowski. "4 of 5 Active Lads to Serve in Cotton Factory." *Rhode Tour.* Rhode Island Historical Society, 2016. Web. 11 July 2016.

3. "Child Labor." *Samuel Slater.* Woonsocket Connection, n.d. Web. 11 July 2016.

4. Stephen Yafa. *Cotton: The Biography of a Revolutionary Fiber.* New York: Penguin, 2005. Print. 165–168.

5. "Burn the Cotton! Memphis, Tenn., May 15, 1862." *Library of Congress.* LOC, 6 Dec. 2013. Web. 11 July 2016.

6. Stephen Yafa. *Cotton: The Biography of a Revolutionary Fiber.* New York: Penguin, 2005. Print. 165–168.

7. Ben Johnson. "Lancashire Cotton Famine." *Historic UK.* Historic UK, 2016. Web. 11 July 2016.

CHAPTER 5. A NEW ERA

1. "Forty Acres and a Mule." *BlackPast.org.* BlackPast.org, 2015. Web. 11 July 2016.

2. Ibid.

3 James C. Giesen. "Sharecropping." *New Georgia Encyclopedia.* Georgia Humanities Council, 26 Jan. 2007. Web. 11 July 2016.

4. "People & Events: Sharecropping in Mississippi." *American Experience.* WGBH Educational, 2009. Web. 11 July 2016.

5. "The Twentieth Century." *Center for World History.* University of California, Santa Cruz, 2007. Web. 11 July 2016.

6. Ben Berntson. "Boll Weevil Monument." *Encyclopedia of Alabama.* Encyclopedia of Alabama, 7 June 2013. Web. 11 July 2016.

Source Notes Continued

CHAPTER 6. COTTON CONTINUES GROWING

1. "Driving Demand for Cotton Jeans." *Cotton Incorporated*. Cotton Incorporated, 2016. Web. 11 July 2016.

2. Hiroko Tabuchi. "A Once-Flourishing Pima Cotton Industry Withers in an Arid California." *New York Times*. New York Times Company, 7 Aug. 2015. Web. 11 July 2016.

3. Ibid.

4. Hiroko Tabuchi. "Chinese Textile Mills Are Now Hiring in Places Where Cotton Was King." *New York Times*. New York Times Company, 2 Aug. 2015. Web. 11 July 2016.

5. John Johnson. "Cotton Seal Celebrates Silver Anniversary." *PCCA*. Plains Cotton Cooperative Association, 1998–1999. Web. 11 July 2016.

6. "Cotton Incorporated." *Reference for Business*. Advameg, 2016. Web. 11 July 2016.

CHAPTER 7. COTTON TODAY

1. "Why Irrigate Cotton?" *Cotton Incorporated*. Cotton Incorporated, 2016. Web. 11 July 2016.

2. Tony Vindell. "New Pickers Put Out Round Cotton Bales Similar to Egg-Laying Chickens." *Raymondville Chronicle News*. Raymondville Chronicle News, 10 Aug. 2011. Web. 11 July 2016.

3. "The Impact of a Cotton T-Shirt." *WWF*. World Wildlife Fund, 16 Jan. 2013. Web. 11 July 2016.

4. Ibid.

5. "Processing the Crop." *Cotton's Journey*. CottonJourney.com, n.d. Web. 11 July 2016.

6. "Cotton Farmers and Workers." *Fairtrade Foundation*. Fairtrade Foundation, 2016. Web. 11 July 2016.

7. Ibid.

CHAPTER 8. COTTON AND THE ENVIRONMENT

1. "Pesticide Use in US Agriculture." US Department of Agriculture. *USDA*, May 2014. Web. 2 Aug. 2016.

2. "Chemical Cotton." *Rodale Institute*. Rodale Institute, 4 Feb. 2014. Web. 11 July 2016.

3. "Cotton Sustainability: Frequently Asked Questions." *Cottoncampus.org*. Cotton Incorporated, 2016. Web. 11 July 2016.

4. "Bt Cotton & Management of the Tobacco Budworm-Bollworm Complex." US Department of Agriculture. *USDA*, Jan. 2001. Web. 11 July 2016.

5. Ibid.

6. "Overview." *WWF*. World Wildlife Fund, 2016. Web. 11 July 2016.

7. "Africa Needs Fair Trade, Not Charity." *YaleGlobal Online*. Yale Center for the Study of Globalization, 2005. Web. 11 July 2016.

8. Will Allen. "Fact Sheet on US Cotton Subsidies and Cotton Production." *Organic Consumers Association*. Organic Consumers Association, Feb. 2004. Web. 11 July 2016.

CHAPTER 9. COTTON'S FUTURE

1. John Davis. "Low-Grade Cotton Brings Top Value in Oil Spill Cleanup." *Texas Tech University*. Texas Tech University, 15 May 2013. Web. 11 July 2016.

2. Ibid.

3. "Innovations." *Cotton Today*. Cotton Incorporated, 2015. Web. 11 July 2016.

4. Hembree Brandon. "New Uses for Cotton: Better Treatments for Wounds." *Delta Farm Press*. Penton, 29 Feb. 2008. Web. 11 July 2016.

5. John Hart. "Cotton Faces Unrelenting Synthetics Competition." *Southeast Farm Press*. Penton, 14 July 2015. Web. 11 July 2016.

6. "History." *Cargill*. Cargill, 2016. Web. 11 July 2016.

7. Ibid.

8. "World Cotton Production." *Monthly Economic Letter*. Cotton Incorporated, July 2016. Web. 9 Sept. 2016.

Index

ABOUT THE AUTHOR

Marcia Amidon Lusted has written 135 books and more than 500 magazine articles for young readers, on topics such as history, biography, science, and literature. She is also an editor, a musician, and a certified permaculturist. She lives in New Hampshire.

BOOK CHARGING CARD

Accession No. _____ Call No. _____

Author _____

Title _____

Date Loaned	Borrower's Name	Date Returned